Hey Kids! Let's Visit London England

Teresa Mills

D1114772

Life Experiences Publishing
Bluff City, Tennessee

Teresa Mills/Life Experiences Publishing
PO Box 53
Bluff City, TN 37618
kid-friendly-family-vacations.com

Book Layout © 2014 BookDesignTemplates.com

Hey Kids! Let's Visit London England/ Teresa Mills.-1st ed.
ISBN 978-1-946049-00-1

Contents

Preface

Welcome

London, England....as the capital of England, London is one of the most visited cities in the country and one of the most popular tourist destinations in the world. Tourists visit because it is rich in culture, history, architecture, arts, music, theater and food!

London includes historical sites such as Westminster Abbey, museums and the Tower of London, as well as the fun attractions like The London Eye, theaters and Kings Cross Station. (Platform 9 3/4 from the Harry Potter movies!)

This book is written as a fun fact guide about the London attractions and sites. The book includes some London history interspersed with fun facts about things to do.

You can visit London right from your own home with this book! You can enjoy this book whether you are preparing for a London vacation with the family and want to learn more about the city, or just enjoy the book and pictures to learn a little more about the famous city.

When you take your family trip to London, I have a free gift for you!

https://kid-friendly-family-vacations.com/londonattractions

Also, take advantage of our companion activity and coloring books to complement this book… available as a set and separately.

https://kid-friendly-family-vacations.com/londonpkg

When you have completed this book, I invite you to enjoy the other books in the series. We visit Washington DC, a Cruise Ship, New York City, San Francisco, Savannah Georgia, Paris France, and Charleston South Carolina.

Enjoy!

Teresa Mills

So… Are you ready? Let's Visit London England!

1

Big Ben

Big Ben is a major landmark in London! Big Ben is the clock tower standing proudly in the city of London near the River Thames. It was first rung in 1859. Since then, the rings from the bells of Big Ben have been a part of London's daily life.

Big Ben is located in the north end of Westminster Palace. It serves as the clock and alarm for the Houses of Parliament. **Big Ben is one of the largest working four faced clock in the world today.** It stands independently making it the one of the tallest clocks in the world. The name, Big Ben, is technically the name of the largest bell inside the clock tower. It is also known as Elizabeth's Tower as a tribute to the Queen.

The tower and clock dials were designed by Augustus Pugin. The dials are 7 meters (about 23 feet) in diameter. The minute hands are 4.2 meters long (about 14 feet) and weigh about 100 kilograms (about 220 pounds). Each number in the clock is 60 centimeter long (almost 2 feet). The light of the clock is illuminated whenever the house of parliament is in session. The belfry, in the topmost part of the clock, contains the five bells.

Big Ben is also a major part of the New Year celebrations in the UK. People count down the end of the year along with the chimes of the tower. When the clock strikes twelve, the tower is lit in fireworks to signal the start of a new year.

Big Ben in London

Fun Facts About Big Ben

- There are several birthdays in the life of Big Ben. The first is on April 10, 1858 when the clock was cast. Then, on May 31, 1859, it began ticking. And finally, on July 11, 1859, Big Ben chimed his first hour.
- Big Ben is the giant bell in the belfry of the Clock Tower at the Palace of Westminster. It supposedly got the nickname after locals just started calling it "Big Ben" and the name stuck. The structure was originally going to be named Victoria after Queen Victoria.
- The Clock is actually run by gravity. There are large weights on long cables that attach to each train of gears. The cables in Big Ben are wound three times per week. Gravity pulls the weights down, rotating the trains. There are three trains (the going, the chiming, and the striking train), each with its own weight.

2

The Red Phone Booth

One of the most famous icons on the streets of London is the red phone booth. These iconic phone booths were designed by Sir Giles Gilbert Scott, a popular architect who also designed landmarks like the Waterloo Bridge and the Liverpool Cathedral.

The red phone booths underwent a series of design changes before they sported the design that is known today. In fact, the very first red telephone booth introduced in 1920 was made of concrete and was painted red and white. A second design made of cast-iron, known as K2, was brought into service in 1926. These K2 models were the first to look much like the red phone booths of today.

The most popular among the different designs is called the Jubilee kiosk, which went into production to honor the fifth jubilee of King George V. Also designed by Scott, these red phone booths were generally smaller versions of the K2. Since these kiosks were smaller in size, it was greatly favored because they were cheaper to produce and required smaller pavement space. Produced in 1936, the Jubilee kiosks replaced most of the earlier red phone booth designs.

What makes these phone booths so iconic is the uniformity. The kiosks manufactured from 1926 featured the Tudor Crown, which was officially used by government offices. It was only in 1953 that Queen Elizabeth II had this crown replaced by the St. Edward's Crown, which symbolizes the actual crown used during British coronations.

The Red Phone Booth

Red Phone Booth in London

Fun Facts About The Red Phone Booth

- The official color of these telephone kiosks is "currant red."
- These kiosks are not only scattered all across the United Kingdom, but can also be found in current and former British colonies like Malta and Gibraltar.
- Sir Giles Gilbert Scott's original color suggestion for the K2 was silver with a green-blue exterior, but the United Kingdom Post Office decided to paint it red to make it easy to spot.
- The original wooden prototype for the K2 is located at the entry of the Royal Academy on Piccadilly.
- In the United Kingdom, there are more than 67,000 red phone booths.

3

Kings Cross

If you are not from London, then you probably first heard about Kings Cross in the Harry Potter movies. In the movies, the characters had to travel to Hogwarts by train. That train leaves from the popular Kings Cross Station. (Well, in a hidden part of that station.)

Kings Cross is also the name of a section in the center of London. Kings Cross belongs to two boroughs; Camden and Islington.

If you are traveling internationally, you will take a train from the St. Pancras terminal of the Kings Cross Station.

For Harry Potter fans out there, you can have your picture taken at the famous platform 9 ¾. This is where Harry took his first travel to the magical world of Hogwarts. They even buried a luggage trolley in the wall to make it look as if a Hogwarts' student has just stepped through the invisible platform door.   Its a pretty cool place to take a picture.

Fun Facts About Platform 9 ¾

- It was made famous by the 1997 publication of Harry Potter.
- Although it is not where the movie is filmed, this simple brown wall is still a wonderful spectacle that Harry Potter fans travel from all over the world to see.
- In addition to the wall that fans take photos of, Kings Cross has recently opened up a Harry Potter store at Platform 9 ¾.   It resembles the Ollivander Wand Shop in the Harry Potter movies, complete with everything from custom wands to butterbeer!

Platform 9 ¾ at Kings Cross

4

Zoo at Regents Park

Regent's Park is located in northwest London. Along the northern side of Regent's Park is the famous London Zoo, also known as Regent's Zoo.

The London Zoo is over 188 years old. That makes it the oldest scientific zoo in the whole world. It houses a total of 17,480 animals and 756 different species, as of 2015. Those numbers earned the London Zoo the distinction of having one of the largest collections of animals in the United Kingdom.

The Zoological Society of London (ZSL) manages the zoo, which was initially used to house animals for scientists to study them. But, fortunately for everybody else, the zoo was opened to the public a long time ago. It was 1847 to be precise. The zoo was recently rebuilt to focus on animal conservation. Along the way, the London Zoo was made better not only for the animals, but for the people visiting the animals.

The London Zoo experience is a little different than other zoos in the world where you can only see the animals from afar. Here, you can actually see many animals like the lemurs, spiders, and lions up close as you walk through special enclosures.

Fun Facts About the Zoo at Regent's Park

- The London Zoo opened on April 27, 1828, almost two weeks after Noah Webster published the first Webster's Dictionary.
- The London Zoo raises Sumatran tigers. These tigers are a critically endangered species. Sumatran tigers have the darkest coats of all species of tigers.
- Harry Potter's chubby cousin, Dudley Dursley, celebrated his birthday in the London Zoo in *Harry Potter and the Philosopher's Stone.*

Giraffes in the Zoo at Regent's Park

5

The London Eye

The London Eye is a cantilevered observation wheel located in London, along the banks of the River Thames. You can see the entire city, even up to Windsor Castle from the London Eye.

It is not a Ferris wheel like you usually see in amusement parks. It is a more sophisticated and high tech construction called an observation wheel. The main difference between the two is that an observation wheel is a more complicated construction than the Ferris wheel. An observation wheel has fixed buses or carriages outside the rim of the wheel, while Ferris wheels have gondolas or carriages that are hanging from the rim.

The London Eye

The London Eye was officially opened in 2000 to celebrate the new millennium. It was initially called The Millennium Wheel. The architects chose a wheel to symbolize the 'turning of the century.' At 442 feet, it was once the tallest wheel in the world.

Did you know that supermodel Kate Moss loves the London Eye so much that she has visited the tourist attraction about twenty-five times (as of this writing)? She is probably the UK celebrity that holds the record for the number of visits to the London Eye. This construction is one of the most popular tourist destinations in London.

The London Eye has thirty-two buses or capsules. The people who constructed this observation wheel must have been superstitious because the number thirteen was skipped. The capsules are numbered from one to thirty-three even though there are only thirty-two capsules. The London Eye can carry 800 people in one rotation, because the capsules resemble a bus.

The London Eye Capsule

Fun Facts About The London Eye

- The London Eye is one of the world's tallest cantilevered observation wheel, not a Ferris wheel!
- The London Eye receives about 3.5 million visitors per year. That's about the same number that visit the Empire State Building in NYC.
- The Eye can take 800 people on a ride at once. That is the same amount of people it would take to fill eleven double-decker buses in London.
- You can see up to forty kilometers in all directions from the top of The London Eye.

6

The Tower of London

The official name of The Tower of London is Her (or His) Majesty's Royal Palace and Fortress. It has served various roles over the years, the most famous being a prison. It has also served as a menagerie, home of the Royal Mint, the home of the Crown Jewels (currently), and formerly a royal residence. Of course, the phrase 'sent to the Tower' is still used as a euphemism to mean imprisonment.

The Tower's history stretches back to the days of Norman rule in England, following William the Conqueror's invasion of 1066. The Tower was merely one of many castles established by the newly arrived Normans. This was a time of unprecedented spree of castle building. The tower served as a castle for most of its early centuries.

The Tower of London

A few years later in 1100, the tower was used as a prison... Bishop Ranulf Flambard, hated by the English for imposing harsh taxes, was imprisoned in the Tower.

The tower never held commoners; it was from its inception a prison for nobles and royals. Most notable of these was the imprisonment of the Princes Edward and Richard in the Tower, and quite likely their murderers. The Tower Of London was not a very secure prison. Roger Mortimer, 1st Earl of March, escaped in 1322 through a hacked hole in his cell wall.

The Tudors didn't care much for the Tower, and so they let it languish. The Tower eventually got a reputation as a dark and foreboding dungeon. If the prisoner was of higher status, he could live in conditions comparable to home. For instance, Sir Walter Raleigh, had rooms in the Tower that were expanded to accommodate his family.

The Yeomen Warders – colloquially, the Beefeaters – take care of the Tower. They provide guided tours, in addition to taking care of the Tower. From the Crown Jewels to the older reaches of the Tower, what was once a prison is now a tourist attraction.

Fun Facts About The Tower of London

- The Tower of London was founded as a palace and a defense system at the end of 1066 by William the Conqueror. It remained a military stronghold until the late 19th century.
- There are over 23,500 jewels at the Tower of London today! The Jewels were moved to the Tower after the Jewel House was destroyed. The total value of the jewels is estimated to exceed £20 billion.
- Twenty-two executions have taken place at the Tower of London over the course of history. The last execution was in 1941 when a man was caught parachuting into England.
- The main key to the tower was stolen in November of 2012. That key is still missing today.

7

The Globe Theater

The old Globe Theater was built by the Lord Chamberlain's Men in 1599, specifically by Richard Burbage. The Lord Chamberlain's Men were William Shakespeare's playing company, which is why the theater is associated with Shakespearean plays. The theatre is called an Elizabethan theater because it was constructed during the Elizabethan period. When the original theater was built, they copied the style of the Roman Coliseum, though it was a much smaller version.

The Shakespeare Globe Theater is also referred to as an amphitheater and can seat more than 1500 people. However, because of the popularity of the plays being held in this theater, and probably because this is the only form of entertainment they had back then, more than 3,000 people would sometimes go and would just linger around the theater and on its grounds.

Did you know that the term 'box office' originated from this period? The people who want to see the plays being held in the theater had to pay the collecting officer. The officer used boxes to collect the payments. Once the payments were collected, the officer would then bring the boxes to a backstage room called the box office.

The old theater was destroyed by fire in 1613, but it reopened again in 1614. It closed permanently in 1642. In 1949, Sam Wanamaker decided to reconstruct the old theater on the same site in Southwark. He was disappointed to find out that the only thing that reminds people of the great Globe Theater that was associated with Shakespeare is a small plaque.

Wanamaker established a charity to be able to come up with the money for the reconstruction. Unfortunately, he died in 1993 before he could see the official opening of the theater to the public in 1994. He was not able to see the 300,000 plus people who visited the site between 1994 and 1996, even though it still was not completely finished.

The Globe Theater

Fun Facts About The Globe Theater

- The Globe originally was able to serve up to 3,000 spectators in its' 100 foot diameter three stories of seating!
- When William Shakespeare was a young writer, he bought shares in the Globe Theater. He owned 12.5% of the theater.
- "Totus mundus agit histrionem", which is Latin for "The whole world is a playhouse" is on a crest above the entrance to the Globe.

8

The Millennium Bridge

The Millennium Bridge is a steel suspension bridge which crosses the River Thames. It is a footbridge, which means that only pedestrians can cross the bridge...no vehicles and no motorcycles.

It was called Millennium Bridge because it was opened on June 10th, 2000. The construction was started in 1998, which means that it only took two years to build the bridge. The British House Estates owns and manages the bridge.

You can find a number of interesting tourist destinations and landmarks at either end of the bridge. On the north end, you will find the majestic St. Paul's Cathedral. You can even see the south portion of the Cathedral while you are crossing the bridge from the south. In fact, the bridge was constructed so that the supports frame the cathedral's façade while the pedestrian is crossing. On the south end, you can find the Globe Theater, Tate Modern, and Bankside Gallery.

The bridge was nicknamed the Wobbly Bridge because it wobbled when people crossed the bridge during the opening. After two days of being open, the management decided to close the bridge to do some structural repairs.   After a couple of years of work, it was reopened in 2002. It still carries the moniker Wobbly Bridge even though it no longer wobbles.

The bridge was built to accommodate 5,000 people at once. When the bridge opened, there were 90,000 people there to celebrate. Up to 2,000 people at any one time crossed the bridge on the opening day.

Like the King's Cross station, the Millennium Bridge was also used by the producers of Harry Potter as the fictional Brockdale Bridge.   The bridge was destroyed by the Death Eaters. This was in the film *Harry Potter and the Half Blood Prince*.

Millennium Bridge

Fun Facts About The Millennium Bridge

- The Millennium Bridge was initially opened on June 10, 2000. It was closed two days later because the pedestrians noticed that the bridge was wobbly. It then re-opened two years later after the motion was eliminated.
- In the 2009 movie *Harry Potter and the Half-Blood Prince*, the bridge was used to represent the Brockdale Bridge that collapses following a dramatic attack by the Death Eaters
- The Millennium Bridge links St Paul's Cathedral on the north bank with Tate Modern and Shakespeare's Globe in Southwark in London. It is London's first dedicated pedestrian footbridge.

9

The Tower Bridge

The Tower Bridge London is not London Bridge. It's very iconic. There's none other that looks like it and it's in London, but that doesn't make it London Bridge. That's the next one up the Thames.

The bridge gets its name from the nearby Tower of London. The bridge itself is one of several bridges over the Thames. This bridge, though, is most likely the most iconic of those bridges.

History

New concerns in the second half of the 19th century required that a new way to cross the River Thames be built downstream of London Bridge. The structure could not be a fixed structure though because of the number of ships traveling the Thames.

So in 1876, a committee was formed to find a solution to this problem. Controversy extended things until a design was finally approved in 1884, submitted by Sir Horace Jones. Construction started two years later, and it was opened on the 30th of June, 1894.

The problem of ships in the river was solved by making the central span a double-leaf bascule. That means that when a ship needs to go through, the structure splits into two pieces and swings both halves up to allow the ships to pass. Though river traffic has declined since the late 19th and early 20th centuries, the bascules are still raised roughly a thousand times per year. That's a bit under three times per day.

The Walkways

The structures linking the two towers above the main bridge-way are walkways, accessible by stair from the towers. From the time of opening until they were closed in 1910, they were a notorious haunt for prostitutes and pickpockets. Because of this, they were little used by regular pedestrians. It was only in 1982 that they were reopened, as part of the Tower Bridge London Exhibition.

The Exhibition itself includes the Great Bridges of the World in the East Walkway.   In the West Walkway is the Cities of the Modern Games. In addition, you can then go on to see the Victorian Engine Rooms, which showcase the original engines used to raise the structure.

The Tower Bridge

Fun Facts About The Tower Bridge

- The Tower Bridge was built in 1886 and it spans the River Thames in London.
- It takes five minutes for each half bascule to be raised on the Tower Bridge for ships to pass.
- There were more than 400 workers involved in building the Tower Bridge. It consists of 70,000 tons on concrete that are deep in the River Thames.

10

St. Paul's Cathedral

St. Paul's Cathedral has been a part of London for three hundred years, and has stood as the tallest building in London from 1710 to 1962. In the UK, only Liverpool Church beats out St. Paul's Cathedral for size.

The Cathedral has hosted the funerals of Lord Horatio Nelson, the Duke of Wellington, and Winston Churchill. It's seen two queens' jubilees and the wedding of Prince Charles and Princess Diana. In addition to all that, it's a working church. Prayers and services take place regularly.

This whole business of size and monumental notability all started after the old St. Paul's Cathedral was burned down during the Great Fire of London in 1666. Since the old cathedral was not particularly well-liked (since it was decaying by that time), the decision was made to build a new cathedral atop the ruins of the old one.

So, on the 30th of July 1669, Sir Christopher Wren – experienced designer of fifty other churches in London – was assigned to design the replacement cathedral. Construction began in June of 1675, and the structure was ready to use by the 2nd of December 1697. The cathedral was consecrated in 1708, and was officially complete on Christmas Day of 1711.

St. Paul's Cathedral

Fun Facts About St. Paul's Cathedral

- In the whispering gallery of St. Paul's Cathedral, you can hear someone whispering from the other side of the gallery 112 feet away!
- The cathedral has been featured in many films such as *Mary Poppins*, *Harry Potter*, and *Sherlock Holmes.*
- St. Paul's dome is 366 feet high - the second largest dome in the world.
- The wedding of Prince Charles and Princess Diana was held at the St. Paul's Cathedral.

11

Westminster Abbey

Westminster Abbey is one of the most well-known churches in the world. Over a million visitors come to see it every year, making it easily one of the most popular tourist attractions in London. Its name, "Westminster", actually means west church.

Westminster Abbey is the traditional place of coronation and burial of English and British monarchs. It was built in the year 960. It was rebuilt in 1517 and then again in the 18th century. It has two towers, ten bells, and a floor area of 32,000 square feet. It features a Gothic design. You can easily notice pointed arches, ribbed vaulting, and flying buttresses.

Westminster Abbey was constructed by Edward the Confessor. Its formal title is "The Collegiate Church of St. Peter, Westminster," since it was built in honor of St. Peter. It was consecrated in December, 1065. As the site of funeral services for members of the royal family, notable royals such as Princess Diana and Queen Elizabeth, the Queen Mother, had their funeral services here. Meanwhile, there have been sixteen royal weddings held in Westminster Abbey since 1100.

Fun Facts About Westminster Abbey

- There is a tomb for "the unknown warrior" in the Abbey. An unknown soldier brought back from France in 1920 was interred in the Abbey to represent the fallen soldiers from the war. Queen Elizabeth, the Queen Mother, started the tradition of laying her bridal bouquet on the tomb of the unknown warrior. Royal brides have followed the practice since then.
- The first king crowned in the Abbey was William the Conqueror. He was crowned on Christmas Day in the year 1066.
- There in an area in the Abbey known as the Poet's Corner, and the first to be buried there was Geoffrey Chaucer, the Father of English Literature, in 1400. The walls

are also lined with statues and memorial plaques to honor England's greatest poets and writers such as Shakespeare, Lord Byron, and Charles Dickens.

Westminster Abbey

12

Buckingham Palace

Popularly known as the home of and administrative headquarters of England's reigning monarch, Buckingham Palace is the location for many state celebrations. It has 775 rooms and has the largest private garden in all of London. It serves not only as a symbol for the British monarchy, but also functions as an art gallery and a popular tourist attraction.

Built in 1705, it used to be the town house of the Duke of Buckingham and was then called Buckingham House. King George III later bought it as a gift for his wife, Queen Charlotte. At that time, it came to be known as "The Queen's House."

The first time the Palace was opened to the public was on August 7, 1993. Over 4,000 people came to see it on its opening day.

Besides having 775 rooms, Buckingham Palace features forty acres of gardens, has a lake and a tennis court, and has a helipad. It has 760 windows, which are cleaned every six weeks.

Buckingham Palace

Fun Facts About Buckingham Palace

- Buckingham Palace became the official Royal Home in 1837. Queen Victoria was the first monarch to live there.
- The floor space of Buckingham Palace is smaller than the Louvre in Paris, but there are still 78 bathrooms!
- There are 775 rooms in Buckingham Palace! Can you imagine cleaning that house?
- Buckingham palace has its own post office!
- A boy named Edward Jones broke into the palace three times. His first break-in was at the age of fourteen, and he was captured by the police.
- There are several secret tunnels under the streets of London that connect Buckingham Palace to other places in the city, like the House of Parliament.

13

Victoria and Albert Museum

The Victoria and Albert Museum in Brompton, named after Queen Victoria and Prince Albert, is the world's largest museum (of applied / decorative arts and design), housing thousands of arts and design pieces. It spans 12.5 acres of land, with 145 galleries containing several million objects. The collection found in the museum includes ancient artwork from around 5,000 years ago up to the present, and comes from all around the world.

The museum was established in 1857 and was originally called South Kensington Museum. It was only in 1899 that it was renamed to Victoria and Albert Museum. Nowadays, it is popularly known as the V&A.

True to being a refuge for arts and design, the building's unique architecture is reflective of that fact. Parts of the museum were built during the Victorian and Edwardian periods, and much of its façade and interiors are still seen today. Notable details include what is known as the Ceramic Staircase by Frank W. Moody, mosaics on the North Façade by Godfrey Sykes, and the Dorchester House fireplace by Alfred Stevens.

The Victoria and Albert Museum is also home to the National Art Library. This library contains a collection of about 750,000 books, photographs, and paintings. It is one of the world's largest decorative arts libraries, and is home to many rare books, letters, and illuminated manuscripts. Notable pieces in the library include papers by Charles Dickens, as well as a collection of comic art like the Krazy Kat Arkive.

Other interesting parts of the V&A Museum are its Cast Courts in the sculpture wing, its contemporary art galleries, and its comprehensive costume collection. Furniture, jewelry, and metalwork are also displayed in the museum.

Victoria and Albert Museum

Fun Facts About The Victoria and Albert Museum

- The Codex Forster, a collection of some of Leonardo da Vinci's notebooks, is housed in the V&A's library.
- The V&A was the first museum to have a public restaurant.
- In 1858, the V&A became the first museum to allow night visits through the use of gas lamps.

14

Piccadilly Circus

Don't be confused; Piccadilly Circus is most assuredly not a circus in the entertainment and performance sense. You won't find a trapeze act, acrobats, or jugglers in Piccadilly Circus. (Except that one time on September 2 of '12 in Piccadilly Circus Circus, hah.)

'Circus' derives from Latin, meaning 'circle' or 'ring'. Piccadilly Circus is, surprisingly enough, reasonably circular. Hence the name fits the place. Like a lot of things in Britain, it's got a fair few years on it, having been built in 1819.

What To Do In The Circus That Isn't A Circus

Memorial Fountain
You could sit at the Memorial Fountain and watch the people going by. In a place like this,

you're bound to see a lot of people to just plain watch.

Of course, there's the fountain itself. It's not quite at the center of Piccadilly Circus, (It's actually on the southwestern side.) but it's where a whole lot of the pedestrian traffic walks past.

Shopping

For those who prefer shopping to people watching, the most prominent store in Piccadilly Circus is Lilywhites, a sporting goods retailer on Regent Street and right next to the fountain. You won't be the first tourist to visit it and certainly not the last, as it's rather popular.   This store offers items on sale quite regularly.

Piccadilly Circus

Fun Facts About Piccadilly Circus

- The street was originally named Portugal Street, but adopted the name Piccadilly Circus during the late 1800's.
- Millions of tourists pass through Piccadilly Circus every year, making the electronic billboards there worth millions in advertising dollars.
- The Piccadilly Circus Tube station is located underneath the Circus itself. It is one of the few stations completely underground.

15

Leicester Square

Leicester Square is surrounded by the Lisle Street, Orange Street, Charing Cross Road, and Whitcomb Street to the north, south, east, and west, respectively. The place is named after the 2nd Earl of Leicester, Robert Sidney. He was a wealthy aristocrat who purchased a large tract of land, (about four acres) which includes this small area which is now known as the Leicester Square.

The earl built a magnificent townhome for himself which he proudly called the Leicester House. The address was initially known as a place where aristocrats live. In fact, Frederick, Prince of Wales, once lived in the Leicester House. The Leicester House later became a museum that housed natural curiosities in the 1780s. In the early 1790s, the place was finally demolished.

Things to do in Leicester Square

- The Square itself has a garden or a small park where you can find several statues and stone busts. You can find the statue of William Shakespeare with dolphins in the middle of the Square. You can also find busts which depict Sir Joshua Reynolds, Sir Isaac Newton, John Hunter, William Hogarth, and most recently, Charlie Chaplin.

- Leicester Square also has several major theaters, namely, Odeon Leicester Square, Odeon Mezzanine, Odeon West End, Empire, and Vue. Odeon Leicester Square hosts a lot of movie premieres not only for British films, but also for American movies. The cinema was also noted as the cinema that used the first digital projector in the whole continental Europe. Vue was formerly known as Warner Brothers Village where Warner Bros films were premiered. Vue purchased the cinema in 2004.

- Visit the Hippodrome. This is not related to hippos or animals. This is a theater built in the 1900s where circus, plays, musicals, and variety shows were performed. The first show in the Hippodrome was performed by Charlie Chaplin. The name

Hippodrome is from animals performing a significant part in a show.

Theater in Leicester Square

Fun Facts About Leicester Square

- Karl Marx lived in Leicester Square in 1848, after many failed German revolutions.
- There are several famous statues on Leicester Square. They include Sir Issac Newton, Charlie Chaplan, and William Shakespeare.
- "Fester Square" is the nickname given to Leicester Square in 1979 when garbage collectors went on strike, and the square was used as a dumping ground.

16

Trafalgar Square

Trafalgar Square is the largest square in London. It is called Trafalgar Square because it commemorates the Battle of Trafalgar. The Battle of Trafalgar showcased a British naval victory over France and Spain in 1805 in Cape Trafalgar, Spain.

The Trafalgar Square was originally designed by John Nash, and then later redesigned by Sir Charles Barry. At the center of it is Nelson's Column, which was named after Admiral Horatio Nelson. He led the British to victory during the Battle of Trafalgar. Nelson's Column is surrounded by four bronze lions. You will also notice that there are some statues and sculptures in the square.

Trafalgar Square originally contained the King's Mews in the 13th century before George IV moved the mews to Buckingham Palace. Nowadays, the square is used for various community gatherings and campaigns.

There are many interesting sites near Trafalgar Square. On the north side is the National Gallery, an art museum that has more than 2,000 paintings. On the east side is the St. Martin in the Fields Church, a famous church built in the 1720s. On the south is Northumberland Avenue. And on the west is The Mall, a road that is closed to traffic on Sundays.

Trafalgar Square

Fun Facts About Trafalgar Square

- A Christmas tree is put up in the square every year. The tree is donated by Norway to show gratitude for England's support during World War II. This practice has been done since 1947.
- The place is famous for its feral pigeons, but people are not allowed to feed them. There is also a hawk trained to keep the pigeons away.
- At the southwest of Trafalgar Square is The Mall, and there is a roadway that leads to Buckingham Palace — the official residence of the royalty in London.
- Trafalgar Square in London was built between 1820 and 1845 as part of a redevelopment of the Charing Cross area.

17

Ben's Cookies

The first Ben's Cookies shop was opened back in 1983 at the Covered Market in Oxford, England. Self-confessed chocolate lover and cookbook author, Helge Rubinstein, created Ben's Cookies, with Karen Brooke Barnett as her co-founder.

Ben's Cookies serve sixteen cookie varieties, including Triple Chocolate Chunk, White Chocolate & Macadamia, Peanut Butter, Oatmeal & Raisin, and Ginger & Dark Chocolate. These cookies are made of 100% natural ingredients.

What makes their cookies even better is that you can eat them shortly after they come out of the oven. They start the day off by making all their dough in a kitchen right outside of Oxford. Each store in England then gets their supply of dough, and then bakes them all day.

Fun Facts About Ben's Cookies

- The man who created the Ben's Cookies logo is the same man who made the drawings on *Charlie and the Chocolate Factory*, *Matilda, Fantastic Mr. Fox*, and fifteen other Roald Dahl books — Quentin Blake.
- Ben's Cookies is named after Rubinstein's son, Ben. The drawing of the cookie-eating boy on their logo is actually Blake's version of the then-young boy.
- Their slogan is "We bake with chunks not chips since 1983." Ben's Cookies uses the best ingredients including chunks — not chips — of delectable UK-made Belgian chocolate.

18

Hampstead Heath

Hampstead Heath is a popular park in the City of London. This popular park is huge. It covers 791 acres of well-kept grass fields, meadows, woodlands, and ponds you can swim in. If you're finding it hard to imagine how huge the park is, consider that one acre is about ¾ the size of an American football field. Now imagine 791 of those.

Hampstead started out as a Saxon village called Hamstede, which is another word for "homestead." From a simple village filled with farmers, Hampstead became the home of the rich, particularly after the plague of 1665. During the 18th century, the place became popular for its natural springs and spas because of their healing properties. Today, there are more than twenty-five of these ponds where people can take a dip and enjoy the water.

The Heath not only houses the rich folks, but also the wildlife. Here you can find rabbits, squirrels, foxes, terrapins, muntjac deer, and grass snakes, among other animals. If you wish to see more, head on to Golders Hill Park. There is a small zoo which houses different creatures such as donkeys, ring-tailed lemurs, and the European Eagle Owls.

Sigmund Freud lived for a year in Hampstead before he passed away in 1939. The house where he stayed is now a museum. Another place to stop by at The Heath is the Kenwood House. This is where the character played by Julia Roberts in *Notting Hill* was filming a movie.

Parliament Hill in Hampstead Heath

Fun Facts About Hampstead Heath

- The Hampstead Tube station is 192 feet below ground. That's the deepest of all the Underground Stations.
- Buried inside the parish church in Hampstead is John Constable, a popular artist back in the day known for his paintings of landscapes.
- Writers and artists find inspiration from the place. The poet John Keats lived in the Wentworth Place (now called Keats House), where he penned *Ode to a Nightingale* while sitting under a tree in the garden.

19

The Tube

Have you taken a ride in the Tube? The Tube is also called the London Underground. It's a high-speed underground railway that allows for travel in Greater London, Buckinghamshire, Essex, and Hertfordshire. It serves 270 stations. The length of its network spans 250 miles. More than a billion people get to ride the Tube every year.

The Tube has been around for more than 150 years. It started operations on January 10, 1863. The trains were originally steam-powered. In 1890, the first deep-level electric railway line was opened. By 1961, the Tube was completely powered by electricity.

While the Tube is currently called London Underground, only 45% of it is actually in tunnels. Its busiest station is Oxford Circus. The earliest trains run at 4:45 A.M. and they run from Oster-ley to Heathrow.

The Tube has been around for a long time. Be-sides helping people move around London easily, it also served as a raid shelter in September, 1940 at the height of World War II. There are al-so many movies that feature the Tube, among them *Skyfall, Sliding Doors*, and *Spectre*.

Why is the Underground called the Tube? That's because of the shape of its tunnels.

Mind the Gap – The Tube

London Tube Station

Fun Facts About The Tube

- The first time a baby was born on the London Underground was in 1924.
- Queen Elizabeth II was the first monarch to ride the Tube. She first rode in 1969 on the Victoria Line.
- The famous American author Mark Twain was one of the first passengers on the Central Line back in 1900.
- The Tube tunnels wind 249 miles through the London Underground.
- The busiest Tube Station in the mornings is the Waterloo Station. More than 57,000 people use that station during the three-hour morning peak.
- The Tube's round blue and red logo is an icon that almost everyone will recognize. It is one of the oldest corporate brands.

20

Harrods

Harrods is a famous luxury department store located on Brompton Road in the Royal Borough of Kensington and Chelsea. It is a seven story building occupying a five acre lot, and has about 330 departments. One of the most eye-catching features of Harrods is its well-preserved façade, which is reminiscent of the late 1800s.

The history of Harrods begins with a twenty-five year old draper named Charles Henry Harrod, who started his own business in 1824 in Southwark, London. By 1834, he was able to open a grocery business in East London, which eventually relocated to Knightsbridge. It was only in 1849 when the business again transferred to a small one-room shop in Brompton, which is now the site of its current store.

Harrod's son, Charles Digby Harrod, was placed in charge in 1861. The store underwent a huge transformation and became one of the most thriving retail stores. By this time, the new store started selling medicine, perfumes, and other luxury items. Since then, Harrods has become the favorite shopping spot of much of London's elite.

The Harrods building, as it is seen today, was finished in 1905, after an eleven year construction. It was designed by renowned architect Charles William Stephens. Since then, Harrods grew into the well-known brand it is today. It now features a retail space of 1,000,000 square feet, covering different shops. The shops include luxury fashion brands, electronics, housewares, and food and drinks. The store is also known for its unique customer services, which includes a personal shopping assistance program and a gift concierge.

Harrods

Fun Facts About Harrods

- Harrods is known to have a strict dress code policy, and has already denied entrance to several people whom they believed weren't appropriately dressed for the store.
- Harrods introduced England's first escalator on November 16, 1898.
- Harrods was a favorite of many famous people, including Charlie Chaplin, Sigmund Freud, and members of the British Royal Family.

21

RAF Museum

The Royal Air Force Museum houses over one hundred aircrafts, including many planes used during the First and Second World Wars. You'll also learn about the different people and events that have shaped the aviation industry and some of the heroic men and women of the Royal Air Force who braved it out during times of conflict.

There are lots of activities you can actually participate in since many of the displays are interactive. You can feel what it's like to fly when you visit the Milestones of Flight and the 3D Cinema. In the Battle of Britain Hall you can visit the *Our Finest Hour* light show. You can also listen to Winston Churchill giving his famous Battle of Britain speech.

Fun Facts About The Royal Air Force Museum

- The Hendon Aerodrome is a place of many firsts, including the first mail delivery via air, first night flight, first parachute dive from a powered aircraft, and the first aerial defense of a city.
- The only place where a life-sized model of the F-35 Lightning II Fighter Jet, aka the F-35 Joint Strike Fighter Jet, is displayed is in the RAF Museum. You may be more familiar with the F-35 as robots in disguise, Breakaway and Thrust, in the *Transformers: Revenge of the Fallen* toy collection. The F-35 has also made an appearance in *The Avengers* and in *Man of Steel*.
- An actual recovered wreck of the Handley Page Halifax II is on display in the Bomber Hall. The Halifax was hit by enemy fire during the raid on Tirpitz and went down in April, 1942. It was recovered in 1973.

22

Warner Brothers Studio

The Warner Bros. Studio is located in Leavesden, Hertfordshire. It is an 80-hectare film and media complex, and is one of the few studios in the United Kingdom where large-scale movies can be produced. The studio complex offers about 50,000 square meters of flexible space for indoor sets, as well as a 32-hectare backlot for exterior sets.

Warner Bros. is a company known for a variety of films and television shows that cater to a large audience. The company was founded on April 4, 1923 by brothers Harry, Albert, Sam, and Jack Warner. Before 1923, the brothers were already engaged in the movie theater business, and even started producing films as early as World War I.

The Warner Bros. Studio in Leavesden was home to the world-famous Harry Potter series for more than 10 years. After filming, the Warner Bros. Studio Tour London decided to open its doors to the public on March 31, 2012 to give the visitors a taste of the wizarding world through its special effects and animatronics. The tour also allows tourists to explore the original sets, including Diagon Alley, the Great Hall, and Dumbledore's office. Since its opening, the studio complex now welcomes around 5,000 visitors per day, and has already won numerous awards.

In addition to the Harry Potter films, the Warner Bros. Studio is also home to a long list of well-known films like *Sherlock Holmes, Inception, Pan,* and *Mission: Impossible*.

Fun Facts About The Warner Brothers Studio

- The area where the studio now stands used to be a prominent airfield and aircraft factory during World War II.
- The first film produced after being converted into a studio was GoldenEye, the 17th movie in the James Bond series.
- The exterior set, which was created to represent Privet Drive in the Harry Potter series, is still visible on Google Maps.
- The Great Hall has no actual ceiling. Camera tricks and CGIs were used in the movie but the actual ceiling is only a small scale model positioned above the camera to make it look as massive as the hall. The hall could fit twenty-two double-decker buses and took over ninety tons (almost 200,000 pounds) of plaster to complete.

23

Stonehenge

One of the world's most famous landmarks is Stonehenge. These standing stones are located on Salisbury Plain in England. According to archaeologists, the first Mesolithic posts in the area were raised in as early as 8500-7000 BC, but it was only in 3000 BC when the first Stonehenge was built. Due to its historical and cultural significance, the site and the surroundings of the Stonehenge were recognized as a World Heritage Site by UNESCO in 1986.

What is fascinating about Stonehenge is how they were built. Archaeologists believe that the boulders were cut into shape by hammering wood into stone. These wooden wedges then expanded when soaked in water, which eventually cut the boulders into smaller pieces. Next, the ancient Britons dug deep circular ditches. Once the ditches were dug up, these stones were made to stand by tying ropes around them and pulling them up. Rocks were then placed to surround the buried part of the stones to keep them in place. This only shows how crafty and talented engineers the ancient Britons were.

There is no written record of how and why the ancient men built Stonehenge, which is why it has sparked several myths and legends. Although it has been widely recognized as an ancient burial site, some historians believe otherwise. Some think that it was built so that the ancient Britons were able to study the movements of the sun and the moon, while others believe it's a sacred healing site.

Stonehenge

Fun Facts About Stonehenge

- Stonehenge used to be private property, and was even auctioned on September 21, 1915. The winner of the auction, Cecil Chubb, decided to give it to the nation three years later.
- Stonehenge is aligned with the midwinter sunset and the midsummer sunset.
- Two stones were used to build Stonehenge: the 25-ton Sarsen stones and the 4-ton bluestones.

24

Duxford Air and Space Museum

Do you know how WWI and WWII airplanes were made? Do you know who built them? If you're dying to know the answers to these questions, then a trip to the Duxford Air and Space Museum or the Imperial War Museum Duxford should be on your to-do list. Or at least convince your mom and dad to take you there.

The IWM Duxford, which opened in 1920, can be found in Cambridgeshire. It houses almost 200 aircrafts and other military vehicles and memorabilia. At the Duxford, you will be introduced to the different personalities who have shaped British aviation. You'll finally get to know the people who designed and built your favorite classic warplanes. One of those brilliant minds is Beatrice Shilling. If not for Shilling's design modification on Merlin engines' carburetor, many aboard Hurricane and Spitfire planes would have perished due to malfunctions. Her accomplishments is just one of the many exhibits in the museum.

There are seven main exhibitions housed in their own building or hangar. There's the AirSpace exhibit, Flying Aircraft, Air and Sea, Battle of Britain Exhibition, Conservation in Action, American Air Museum, and the Land Warfare Hall. Make sure to visit each one to get your fill of British aviation history.

Another thing to watch out for in Duxford is the air show. The dazzling display of aircrafts and piloting skills have been one of the main attractions since 1973. They are held regularly on its still active airfield.

Fun Facts About Duxford Air and Space Museum

- IWM Duxford is Britain's largest aviation museum.
- Many of the buildings and hangars in the Duxford Museum have been around since World War I. In fact, many of them are still operational.
- One of the aircrafts prominently displayed at the Duxford is the Spitfire, which is famous for its rounded wing tips. The Lockheed SR-71 Blackbird in the American Air Museum is the only one of its kind exhibited outside the United States. Jetfire in *Revenge of the Fallen* transforms into a SR-71.

I hope you enjoyed visiting London. Now let's head across the pond to the USA to visit Chicago where we will learn about a museum guarded by two bronze lions and an 18 mile lakefront trail!

https://kid-friendly-family-vacations.com/booktour-visitchicago

----

Sign up for my newsletter for all upcoming up-dates as well as some free gifts.

https://kid-friendly-family-vacations.com/londonattractions

Rather visit the eastern USA? Hop a flight to New York City to find out about a building that looks like an iron and a beach amusement park a short subway ride from downtown Manhattan!

https://kid-friendly-family-vacations.com/booktour-visitnyc

Learn more about the entire Hey Kids! Let's Visit series!

https://kid-friendly-family-vacations.com/booktour-series

Please leave a review to help others lean more about London whether traveling or learning from home.

https://kid-friendly-family-vacations.com/review-london

MORE FROM KID FRIENDLY FAMILY VACATIONS

BOOKS

Books to help build your kids / grandkids life experiences through travel and learning

https://kid-friendly-family-vacations.com/books

COLORING AND ACTIVITY PAGKAGES

Coloring pages, activity books, printable travel journals, and more in our Etsy shop

https://kid-friendly-family-vacations.com/etsy

RESOURCES FOR TEACHERS

Resources for teachers on Teachers Pay Teachers

https://kid-friendly-family-vacations.com/tpt

It is our mission to help you build your children's and grand-children's life experiences through travel. Not just traveling with your kids... building their "Life Experiences"! Join our community here: https://kid-friendly-family-vacations.com/join

Acknowledgments

Proof-reading / Editing

Marcia Reagan at ProofRaiders

Cover Photos

Trafalgar Square – © galdolfos / deposit photos

All others – Personal vacation photos

Photos in Book

Big Ben – © artsy / deposit photos

Red Phone Booth – personal vacation photo

Red Phone Booth (2nd) – © kmiragaya / deposit photos

Platform 9 ¾ - © chrisdorney / deposit photos

Zoo at Regent's Park - © Pashmina Parikh – 123rf.com

London Eye – 2 personal vacation photos

Tower of London – personal vacation photo

Globe Theater – personal vacation photo

Millennium Bridge - © paulfleet / deposit photos

Tower Bridge – personal vacation photo

St Paul's Cathedral – personal vacation photo

Westminster Abbey – © masterlu / deposit photos

Victoria and Albert Museum - © chrisdorney – deposit photos

Buckingham Palace – personal vacation photo

Piccadilly Circus – © irstone / deposit photos

Leicester Square – personal vacation photo

Trafalgar Square – © galdolfos / deposit photos

Hampstead Heath - © RubinowaDama / deposit photos

The Tube (mind the gap) - © Thomas Dutour / 123rf.com

Tube Station - © Elena Elisseeva / 123rf.com

Harrods – © jorgefelix / deposit photos

Stonehenge – personal vacation photo

ABOUT THE AUTHOR

Teresa Mills is the bestselling author of the "Hey Kids! Let's Visit..." Book Series for Kids!

Teresa's goal through her books and website is to help parents / grand-parents who want to build the life experiences of their children / grand-children through travel and learning activities.

She is an active mother and Mimi. She and her family love traveling in the USA, and internationally too! They love exploring new places, eating cool foods, and having yet another adventure as a family! With the Mills, it's all about traveling as family.

In addition to traveling, Teresa enjoys reading, hiking, biking, and helping others.

Join in the fun at kid-friendly-family-vacations.com

Made in the USA
Coppell, TX
15 November 2022

86405740R00059